W9-CRW-310

Forest Park
Elementary School

Elizabeth Blackwell

92-81-115

PIONEER DOCTOR

MATTHEW G. GRANT

Illustrated by John Nelson

GALLERY OF GREAT AMERICANS SERIES

★ ★★★★★★★★★★★★★★★★★★★★★★★★ ★

Elizabeth Blackwell

PIONEER DOCTOR

MATTHEW G. GRANT

Illustrated by John Nelson

Text copyright © 1974 by Publication Associates. Illustrations copyright © 1974 by Creative Education. International copyrights reserved in all countries. No part of this book may be reproduced in any form without written permission from the publisher. Printed in the United States.

Library of Congress Number: 73-15858   ISBN: 0-87191-307-0

Published by Creative Education, Mankato, Minnesota 56001

LIBRARY OF CONGRESS CATALOGING IN PUBLICATION DATA
Grant, Matthew G
    Elizabeth Blackwell.
    (His Gallery of great American series. Women of America)
    SUMMARY: An easy-to-read biography of Elizabeth Blackwell who overcame many difficulties
to become the first woman physician in the United States.
    [1. Blackwell, Elizabeth, 1821-1910.   2. Women physicians.   3. Physicians.]
I. Nelson, John, illus.   II. Title.
R154.B623G7   610'.92'4 [B] [92]   73-15858
ISBN 0-87191-307-0

CONTENTS

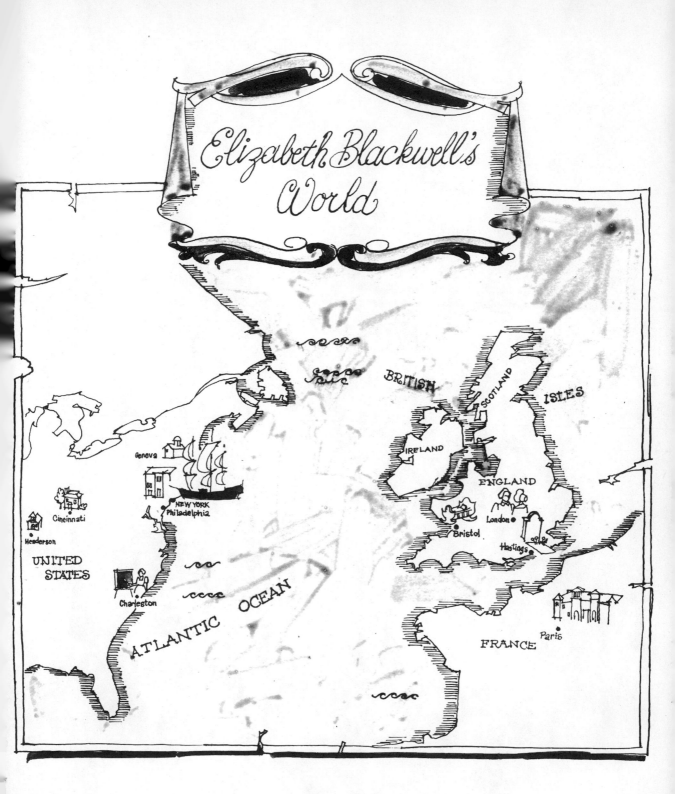

Elizabeth Blackwell's World

FINDING A NEW LIFE

Little Elizabeth crouched by the upstairs window. Outside, a riot was raging. Shouting men roamed the streets of Bristol, England. Burning buildings lit up the night sky. Elizabeth was afraid.

Later, her father came home and tried to tell her why the riot had happened. "Poor people are hungry. They feel our government is unjust toward them, and they think their only hope is violence."

Samuel Blackwell was a rich sugar merchant. But he was also a deep-thinking man. He wished to help the suffering poor but he did not know how. His nine children shared his beliefs.

It was the year 1830. Before too long, the Blackwell family found out what it was like to be poor. Mr. Blackwell's business failed. He said:

"We will go to America and start over again."

Elizabeth clung to the hand of her little sister, Emily, as they got on board a sailing ship. She tried to be brave as the shore of England disappeared and gray waves surged all around them.

The poorest passengers, deep in the ship's hold, took sick. Several died. Elizabeth watched with horror as the bodies were brought up, prayed over, and dropped into the sea. Her father said: "They died because they were poor. They had to travel in a dark, filthy hold. All over the world, people die needlessly because they are poor. Somehow, we must find a way to help them."

Eleven-year-old Elizabeth nodded.

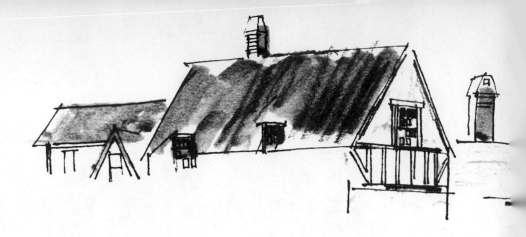

Mr. Blackwell started a new sugar business in New York. But his conscience got in the way of his making a living. This happened because sugar was grown by slaves.

"Black slaves deserve to be free!" said Blackwell. "How can I carry on a business that is founded upon human misery?" But it was the only business he knew. Once more he failed to prosper. In 1837 he took the family to Cincinnati, Ohio. Not long after, Samuel Blackwell died.

A WOMAN'S WORK

Elizabeth Blackwell, aged 16, had to go to work. Unlike most well-to-do young women of the time, she had been well educated. So she became a teacher in Kentucky. Despite her youth, she was forceful and determined to succeed.

15

Elizabeth was impatient when men talked about how "inferior" women were. She, like many other women of that time, was becoming aware of women's rights.

Was not one of those rights the right to earn a good living? Even the best woman teacher earned far less than a man. Wasn't her mind as good as that of any man she knew? Of course it was! If only men would give women a chance to prove themselves!

The years went by. She felt she was wasting her life. Then, when she was 24, she happened to visit a friend named Mary who was dying.

Mary took Elizabeth's hand. "The worst of my illness is being treated by a gruff, unfeeling doctor. If only there were women doctors!"

Elizabeth agreed. And then her friend said: "You are young and strong. You could become a doctor."

OPENING DOORS

It was impossible! Women did not become doctors. But Elizabeth could not forget her dying friend's words. For weeks she thought about it. Then she announced to her family: "I am going to try to become a doctor."

Elizabeth had great difficulty finding a place to study. No medical school would admit a woman. So she studied privately at first, helped by Quaker doctors who believed in women's rights.

In 1847 she applied to Geneva Medical College, a small school in New York. Largely as a joke, the school admitted her. The teachers and students waited for her to make a fool of herself and quit.

In those days, "nice" women fainted at the sight of blood. They never talked about the workings of the body. But Elizabeth was not silly. She felt she could learn anything a

FRONT ST.

man could learn—and she proved it. Students who had laughed at her began to respect her courage and her fine mind. The jokes stopped —but the townspeople of Geneva were sure she was some kind of indecent woman. No one in town would speak to her.

During her summer vacation, she helped treat the sick at Philadelphia's huge Blockley Almshouse. The most miserable of the sick poor came to this place. Elizabeth found out how truly ignorant she was as she tried to help them. "I must learn more!" she said. "There is so much work to be done among the sick. Somehow, I must get other women to help me!"

That fall, she returned to school.

At that time, a medical degree required only a short period of study. Elizabeth Blackwell became a doctor of medicine on January 23, 1849. She was the first woman physician to graduate in the United States.

She went to Paris to learn more about the diseases of women and children. While treating a sick baby, she was infected with an eye disease. It caused her to lose the sight of one eye.

She needed a lot of courage in the weeks that followed. She suffered pain and self-doubt as well.

She went to England and became a friend of the famous nurse, Florence Nightingale. In 1850 she received good news. Lydia Folger had become the first American-born woman doctor—and other women were seeking medical degrees. Even Emily, Elizabeth's younger sister, wanted to become a doctor.

FOUNDER OF A HOSPITAL

Dr. Elizabeth Blackwell returned to New York in 1851. Her great desire was to help the sick poor. But at first, she was not able to practice medicine. People were still very prejudiced against a woman doctor.

Little by little, women patients came to her. She became used to their saying: "Why, you are a proper doctor after all!"

In 1853 she opened a dispensary, a kind of clinic, for treating poor women and children. She was joined in this work by her sister Emily, who graduated from medical school the following year. The two women begged their wealthy friends to help them start a real hospital.

Elizabeth and Emily Blackwell's dream came true in 1857, when the New York Infirmary for Women and Children opened its doors. It was the first true hospital for women, run by women doctors, anywhere in the world.

Not only did the hospital treat the poor, but it also trained nurses. A black woman doctor, Rebecca Cole, joined the staff and set

up the first "visiting doctor" service ever known in a large American city.

In 1868, the Infirmary opened its own medical college for women. Then Elizabeth received a letter from England, begging her to come there and "do for the women of England what you have done in America." She left the Infirmary in the capable hands of Emily and returned to the land of her birth in 1869. There she lived and worked for another 40 years, a champion of women's rights. She died May 31, 1910.

GALLERY OF GREAT AMERICANS SERIES

INDIANS OF AMERICA
- GERONIMO
- CRAZY HORSE
- CHIEF JOSEPH
- PONTIAC
- SQUANTO
- OSCEOLA

EXPLORERS OF AMERICA
- COLUMBUS
- LEIF ERICSON
- DeSOTO
- LEWIS AND CLARK
- CHAMPLAIN
- CORONADO

FRONTIERSMEN OF AMERICA
- DANIEL BOONE
- BUFFALO BILL
- JIM BRIDGER
- FRANCIS MARION
- DAVY CROCKETT
- KIT CARSON

WAR HEROES OF AMERICA
- JOHN PAUL JONES
- PAUL REVERE
- ROBERT E. LEE
- ULYSSES S. GRANT
- SAM HOUSTON
- LAFAYETTE

WOMEN OF AMERICA
- CLARA BARTON
- JANE ADDAMS
- ELIZABETH BLACKWELL
- HARRIET TUBMAN
- SUSAN B. ANTHONY
- DOLLEY MADISON